Saniyah Goes to the Zoo

By

Saniyah Dawson and Scott P. Dawson

The day had finally come. It was the fisrt day
of summer camp and Saniyah could hardly wait.

1

Saniyah was so excited she was up before her alarm clock went off. She made up her bed and brush her teeth. Took a bath and made something to eat for herself, her dad, and her dog Marine.

Today was field trip day at Summer Camp and Saniyah told her dad all the animals she wanted to see at the Zoo. Her dad asked if she was nervous to meet the new kids at summer camp and Saniyah replied, "Not at all!" She was excited to make new friends. Saniyah gave her dad a hug and kiss as she left to go off to summer camp.

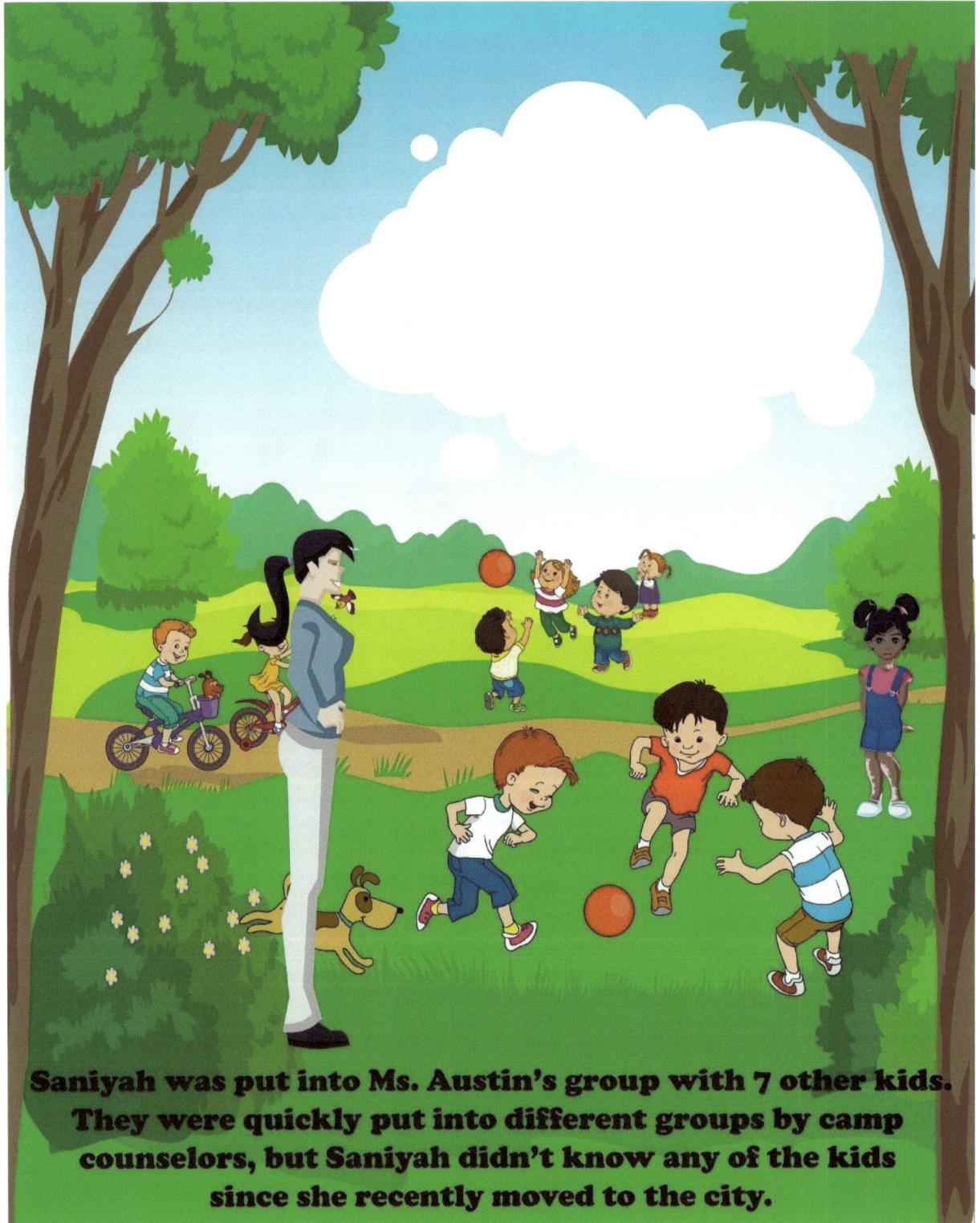

Saniyah was put into Ms. Austin's group with 7 other kids.
They were quickly put into different groups by camp
counselors, but Saniyah didn't know any of the kids
since she recently moved to the city.

After getting on the bus to the zoo one of the other kids named Randy Turned around in his seat and asked Saniyah what was wrong with her skin. Saniyah replied nothing was the matter, but she has Vitiligo and that can sometimes change her skin color though it isn't harmful. Randy, tried to pronounce Vitiligo and became frustrated and embarrassed because he couldn't say the word.

To hide his embarrassment, Randy yelled out to the other kids,"Hey look this girl is dirty and has the cooties!" Saniyah became sad and embarrassed and wondered why Ms. Austin didn't stop Randy from making fun of her, but Ms. Austin was all the way in the front of the bus and couldn't hear much over the kids loud playing and laughter.

Saniyah sunk low in her seat and looked out her window thinking about her friends she had left behind where she used to live. Things weren't going well for Saniyah. Randy kept making fun of her skin and the kids kept laughing. After arriving at the Zoo, Saniyah didn't care too much about seeing all the animals she told her dad about earlier; she was just ready to go home.

Ms. Austin took the kids into the Animal Kingdom section of the Zoo and allowed the kids to wander around. Saniyah was walking slowly behind everyone because she was trying to stay as far away from Randy's hurtful jokes. She eventually found a quiet corner where none of the kids were, sat on the ground, and started to cry. The other kids were busy making fun of the monkeys so none of them had even realized Saniyah was not with the group.

Saniyah heard, "Pssst. What's wrong?" She looked around,
but didn't see anyone. The voice said, "Up here!" when
Saniyah looked up she saw this gigantic giraffe looking
over the fence at her and she couldn't believe
the giraffe was talking to her.
The giraffe said, "My name is Lisa, what's yours?"
Saniyah told Lisa her name. Lisa then asked,
"Why are you crying? Are you lost?"

Saniyah explained that she didn't have any friends and that she's new to the city. She also shared that Randy kept making fun of her skin. Lisa asked, "Why is Randy making fun of your skin?" Saniyah replied, "Because it's different from him and the other kids'." Lisa said "Oh. Saniyah, that's a good thing! Our differences are what make us special. " Lisa then told Saniyah to wait there because she wanted her to meet her friends.

When Lisa came back, she introduces Saniyah to her friends.
Lisa said, "This is my friend
Eddie who is a Zebra, my friend Katie who is a
Peacock, and Bobby who is a cheetah." They all said, "Nice to
meet you Saniyah."
Bobby then said, "Lisa told us about your problem with a bully
and we'd like to help you."

Lisa asked Saniyah, "What do you notice about each one of us?" Saniyah said, "You're all animals." Lisa and the gang all laughed. She said, "Guilty but that's not what I meant. What do you see about our skin?" Saniyah replied, "They're all different colors." Lisa, said, "Correct! We all are different and that's what makes us special; there's nothing wrong with any of us. Because our differences makes us special, people come from near and far to see us. Be proud that you are different because that makes you special."

Randy came around the corner and saw Saniyah
talking to the animals.
He began to laugh and said, "Now you can speak to the
animals too? You really are weird".
Saniyah looked at her new friends and said,
"Everyone, meet Randy."
Randy started to laugh again until the animals said,
"Hello Randy. We've heard a lot about you."

Randy stopped laughing and became afraid because the animals
were actually talking and they knew his name.
Bobby told Randy that being a bully is not a nice thing and
that just because people are different
doesn't mean you should make fun of them.
Eddie asked Randy to be nicer to Saniyah because
there's nothing wrong with her skin,
and making fun of her hurts her feelings. Randy said, "I'm sorry
Saniyah I didn't know I was hurting your feelings"
and he promised the animals the he would be nicer.

Just then, the other kids came around the corner and saw Randy talking to the animals. They all laughed at Randy and called him weird for thinking that he could talk to animals. Randy was embarrassed and understood, in that moment, how he had made Saniyah feel. Saniyah defended Randy and said, "Leave him alone. We were just talking with our new friends." The kids laughed even harder.

Saniyah then said, "Class, meet Eddie, Lisa, Katie, and Bobby." The animals all said, "Hey Y'all!", and the kids went running and screaming away. That made Randy and Saniyah laugh.

For the rest of the field trip Randy and Saniyah were becoming good friends. Randy had apologized to Saniyah for being a bully and thanked her for defending him.

When Saniyah's father came to pick her up from Summer Camp he asked her how her day was. Saniyah replied, "Great! I saw all my favorite animals and I met a new friend. I can't wait to go back tomorrow."

The End

Keep on the lookout for more
adventures with Saniyah

A portion of the proceeds from this book series goes towards the Nspired Ascensions Inc. Scholarship fund and other organizations helping others. If you'd like to contribute to our organization or make any type of donation, please visit our website.

Nspired Ascensions Inc.
www.nspiredascension.com

www.ingramcontent.com/pod-product-compliance
Lightning Source LLC
Chambersburg PA
CBHW041243040426
42445CB00004B/129